I0606343

Bird Behavior

BY ANGELA LIM

An Imprint of Abdo Publishing
abdobooks.com

abdobooks.com

Printed in the United States of America, North Mankato, Minnesota.
052023
092023

Cover Photo: David Ryo/Shutterstock Images
Interior Photos: Rafael Berlandi/Shutterstock Images, 4–5; VH-studio/Shutterstock Images, 6; Shutterstock Images, 7, 9, 12–13, 20–21, 23, 24 (bottom left), 29 (top); Iliana Arredondo/Shutterstock Images, 10; Ekaterina Staromanova/Shutterstock Images, 14; Elena Karetnikova/Shutterstock Images, 16; Christine Bird/Shutterstock Images, 19; Africa Studio/Shutterstock Images, 24 (top left); iStockphoto, 24 (top right); Mayer Kleinostheim/Shutterstock Images, 24 (bottom right); Elizaveta Galitckaia/Shutterstock Images, 26; Sutthiphong Chandaeng/Shutterstock Images, 28; Vincenzo Iacovoni/Shutterstock Images, 29 (bottom)

Editor: Arnold Ringstad
Series Designer: Katharine Hale

Library of Congress Control Number: 2022949076

Publisher's Cataloging-in-Publication Data

Names: Lim, Angela, author.
Title: Bird behavior / by Angela Lim
Description: Minneapolis, Minnesota: Abdo Publishing Company, 2024 | Series: Animal behavior | Includes online resources and index.
Identifiers: ISBN 9781098291006 (lib. bdg.) | ISBN 9781098277185 (ebook)
Subjects: LCSH: Birds--Behavior--Juvenile literature. | Birds--Juvenile literature. | Ornithology--Juvenile literature.
Classification: DDC 591.51--dc23

CONTENTS

The Amazon parrot is a popular pet.

What Does Suzy Want?

Owen was playing a game on his phone. Suddenly his pet Amazon parrot, Suzy, let out a loud chirp. Owen looked up at Suzy. She flapped her wings and looked at him.

Owen walked toward Suzy's cage in the corner of the room.

A parrot that feels playful and friendly may sit on its owner's shoulder.

He studied the bright-green parrot. He wondered what Suzy wanted. He looked into the bird's eyes. He noticed that his pet's pupils kept growing and shrinking. Owen knew this

Watching a bird's eyes can help reveal its mood.

was called eye flashing and eye pinning. The bird looked relaxed.

Suzy cocked her head at Owen. She clicked her tongue and chirped again. Suzy also flicked her tail up and down.

Owen thought about what these sounds and actions meant. He realized Suzy wanted to play! He got his mom to open the cage. Suzy flew out and landed on Owen's shoulder. She rubbed against him and let out a happy purr.

What Is Behavior?

People talk about their feelings. They smile when they are happy. They cry when they are sad. Animals have feelings too. They communicate their **emotions** through their behavior. Behavior lets animals of the same **species** communicate with one another. These behaviors also help people better understand animals.

Behavior Changes

An owner should pay attention to a sudden change in a bird's behavior. It may signal that the bird needs something. For example, a bird may scream if it is bored. It is important to have toys such as blocks and ropes for birds to play with.

Making noise is one way that birds can communicate their feelings.

Birds react to their surroundings in many ways. They look, act, and sound different when they are happy, stressed, or bored. Their **postures** may change if they are scared.

Birds sometimes hang upside down if they feel comfortable and safe.

Their tail and head movements show their emotions. They may chirp or make other sounds to attract attention.

Birds may not show the same behaviors as people. But behaviors can help birds communicate with their owners. They alert the owners to their needs. Bird owners must understand their pets' behaviors. This lets the owners provide the best care for their pets.

Primary Source

Bird expert Alyson Kalhagen talked about some of the behaviors birds may show:

> Is the bird squawking, lunging, hissing, head-bobbing, fluffing its feathers, or otherwise changing its [behavior] in addition to the eye pinning? . . . Look for patterns in your bird's responses . . . to help you determine what the bird is feeling.

Source: Alyson Kalhagen. "What Is Bird Eye Pinning?" *Spruce Pets*, 23 Sept. 2019, thesprucepets.com. Accessed 7 June 2022.

What's the Big Idea?

Read this quote carefully. What is its main idea? Explain how the main idea is supported by details.

The position of a cockatoo's crest can show other birds how it is feeling.

CHAPTER 2

How Birds Communicate

Birds use a wide variety of sounds to communicate. For example, parrots squawk when they are excited. Zebra finches chirp when they are happy. Birds also communicate with visual cues. Cockatoos have a crest of feathers on top of their heads.

Birds have many ways to communicate with each other in the wild.

Raised feathers are a sign of excitement. Flat feathers are a sign of fear. Birds may move their heads, flap their wings, or spread their tails to communicate.

Some behaviors have multiple meanings. Eye pinning and eye flashing can mean the bird is excited, angry, or scared. Some parrots purr when they are happy or when they are stressed. Owners should look at the bird's body language to determine how it is feeling.

Signs a Bird Is Stressed

Bird owners can listen for sounds to know about the mood of their pets. African gray parrots may growl when they are feeling unfriendly. Parrots may scream if they are unhappy or bored. Cockatoos may click their beaks several times when stressed. Parrots are talkative birds. If they become more quiet than usual, they may be unhappy.

Owners should listen carefully to their birds to tell if they are stressed.

Visual cues can also show stress. A stressed bird may have a **rigid** posture. It may spread its tail feathers. It may have its head down. Eye pinning can be another sign of stress.

Feeling Friendly

Birds use sounds to show when they are feeling friendly. A happy bird chirps and sings. It may click its tongue to get its owner's attention.

Regurgitation

A bird sometimes regurgitates food. This means partially digested food comes out of the bird's mouth. People may find this behavior gross. But it is actually a way that a bird shows love! A bird feeds regurgitated food to its young or its mate.

A bird also uses its appearance to show when it is feeling playful. It has a relaxed posture. It may bob its head and flip its tail. It may flap its wings when it is happy. Some birds even hang upside down when they feel safe.

Further Evidence

Look at the website below. Does it give any new evidence to support Chapter Two?

Do Birds Talk When They Squawk?

abdocorelibrary.com/bird-behavior

Flapping its wings may show that a bird is happy.

Birds that are relaxed and happy are more willing to play.

CHAPTER 3

Caring for a Pet Bird

Bird owners need to understand the behaviors of their birds. A happy bird may chirp. If the bird is relaxed, then it can be held and played with.

A bird owner must be aware of unfriendly behavior. This includes spread-out tail feathers. Owners know not to handle the bird if it shows this behavior. A bird may bite or act aggressively if it is stressed or scared. Owners should check the bird's **environment**. They can try to figure out why the bird is stressed. Long-term stress can cause health problems in birds.

Signs of Illness

Some bird behaviors can be signs of illness. Birds fluff their feathers when they are cold. If feathers are fluffed for a long time, it may mean the bird is sick. A bird's wings may droop if the animal is tired or feels unwell.

Expert trainers can share their experience and knowledge with pet bird owners.

Bird Training

Pet birds may bite or scream when they are stressed. These behaviors can be frustrating.

Improving Mood

A healthy diet

A large cage

A quiet space

Toys to play with

A pet bird may be stressed if its needs are not met. Its mood improves when it is properly cared for.

Pet owners should make sure that the birds' needs are being met.

Owners can take steps to prevent biting. They should not pick up stressed birds. Owners should remain calm if bitten. They should not yell at their birds. Yelling can sound like squawking, which is a way for birds to communicate excitement.

Parrot owners often report that their birds scream. This behavior is normal at dawn and **dusk**. But it can be a sign of boredom during the day. Owners should make sure that their birds have toys to play with. They should make sure that the pets have time outside of their cages. A quiet house can reduce a bird's stress.

Understanding bird behavior helps owners have a good relationship with their birds.

Training a bird not to bite or scream takes time. Owners who understand bird behavior know when to play with their pets. They know when their pets need space. Owners should respect the moods of their birds. They can have a healthy relationship with their pets.

Barbara Heidenreich is an animal trainer. She talked about some ways to keep a pet bird happy:

> You can't just leave a bird in [its] cage all day. Birds are social creatures. . . . It's nice to have them in an environment [in] which you think you're going to be able to interact with them.

Source: "Are You Ready to Adopt a Bird?" *PetMD*, 28 Dec. 2018, petmd.com. Accessed 7 July 2022.

Comparing Texts

Think about the quote. Does it support the information in this chapter? Or does it give a different perspective? Explain how in a few sentences.

Body Language

Crest down

Rigid posture

Stressed Behaviors

Playful Behaviors

Head bowing

Singing and chirping

Glossary

dusk
the period of time right before night

emotions
strong feelings, such as excitement or stress

environment
the surroundings in which a person or animal lives

posture
a body position

rigid
stiff or inflexible

species
a group of animals or plants of the same kind

Online Resources

To learn more about bird behavior, visit our free resource websites below.

Visit **abdocorelibrary.com** or scan this QR code for free Common Core resources for teachers and students, including vetted activities, multimedia, and booklinks, for deeper subject comprehension.

Visit **abdobooklinks.com** or scan this QR code for free additional online weblinks for further learning. These links are routinely monitored and updated to provide the most current information available.

Learn More

Birds of North America. DK, 2022.

Murray, Julie. *Parrots.* Abdo, 2020.

Perdew, Laura. *Birdbrain: Are Birds Dumb?* Abdo, 2022.

Index

About the Author

Angela Lim is a writer and editor. She lives in Minnesota.